Ghost LINERS

First published in 1998 in the United States by
Little, Brown and Company
3 Center Plaza
Boston, Massachusetts 02108
U.S.A.

Library of Congress Cataloging-in-Publication Data

   Ballard, Robert D.
   Ghost Liners / by Robert D. Ballard and Rick Archbold;
   paintings by Ken Marschall. — 1st ed.
   p.   cm.
   Summary: Depicts five famous ships that have been lost at sea in modern times,
   the Empress of Ireland, the Lusitania, the Andrea Doria, the Britannic, and the
   Titanic.
   ISBN 0-316-08020-9
   1. Shipwrecks—Juvenile literature. 2. Shipwrecks—Pictorial works—Juvenile
   literature. 3. Ocean liners—Juvenile literature. 4. Sea stories—Juvenile literature.
   [1. Shipwrecks. 2. Ocean liners. 3. Sea stories.] I. Archbold, Rick, 1950-   .
   II. Marschall, Ken, ill. III. Title.
   G525.B2557 1998   98-3412
   910.4'52—dc21

Endpapers: *Titanic* leaving Southampton.
Previous page: *Alvin* explores the severed bow section of the *Titanic*.
Opposite: *Delta* illuminates the *Lusitania's* anchor.
Pages 4–5: *Alvin's* light shines on the *Titanic's* starboard side.

Produced by
Madison Press Books
40 Madison Avenue
Toronto, Ontario, Canada
M5R 2S1

10 9 8 7 6 5 4 3 2 1

Printed in Singapore

Ghost LINERS

EXPLORING THE WORLD'S GREATEST LOST SHIPS

BY ROBERT D. BALLARD AND RICK ARCHBOLD • ILLUSTRATIONS BY KEN MARSCHALL

Historical consultants: Don Lynch, Simon Mills, Mark Reynolds and Eric Sauder

A MADISON PRESS BOOK

Produced for

LITTLE, BROWN AND COMPANY

Boston   New York   Toronto   London

Contents

From *Titanic* to *Britannic*

August 29, 1995

The Mediterranean sun was already hot when I clambered down into the U.S. Navy's smallest nuclear-powered submarine, *NR-1*, as it bobbed gently on the sea swells. Our research ship had just arrived at the wreck of the *Britannic*, and I couldn't wait to get my first look at the *Titanic*'s younger sister. The *Britannic* was one of the *Titanic*'s two almost-identical twins. The older sister, the *Olympic*, lived a long and useful life, but the *Britannic* served for only eleven months. Originally to be called the *Gigantic*, its name was changed after the *Titanic* went down.

The date was August 29, 1995. In just three days, on September 1, we would mark the tenth anniversary of our discovery of the most famous shipwreck in history — the *Titanic*. Since then my whole life had changed. I had spent much of the last decade exploring the wrecks of famous ships, ghost liners, but none would ever compare with the sheer excitement of finding the *Titanic*.

The *NR-1* may be the smallest nuclear sub in the world, but it is very different from *Alvin*, the tiny three-person submarine we used in 1986 to explore the *Titanic* wreck. (They are about as similar as a space capsule and the shuttle.) *NR-1* is 150 feet (45 meters) long and carries a crew of eleven people. There's enough room to walk around

(Above far left) The headlights of our submarine *NR-1* pierce the twilight world of the *Britannic* wreck.
(Above left) Inside the submarine, I prepare to take a photograph through one of the viewports.
(Above right) On the bridge of *NR-1*, we watch the video screens as the sub moves closer to the wreck of the *Titanic*'s sister.
(Pages 8–9) As distress rockets shoot skyward, lifeboats pull away from the sinking R.M.S. *Titanic*.

but you can see more on *NR-1*'s video screens than through its three tiny windows, so you don't have to crouch on your knees for hours to see out, as we did in *Alvin*.

But some things don't change, whether the submarine is big or small. Once you've sunk below the surface, there is the same sense of stepping outside time and entering a completely alien world. On this trip, I would be underwater for a day and a half. In fact, because the *NR-1* is nuclear-powered, it could stay submerged for a month if necessary.

Once we'd reached a position a few feet above the bottom, we located the *Britannic* on sonar and began moving toward the wreck. I stood behind *NR-1*'s pilot and watched the video screens. The water was amazingly clear, and the sub's powerful headlights lit up the underwater gloom, but all I could see was a fish swimming lazily by. Then slowly, a massive

black wall began to materialize in front of us. As we came closer, I could see the lines where the steel plates that made up the hull overlapped and the rivets that still held them together. It was as if someone had built a vast steel barrier underwater. The *Britannic* rests on its side, so what we were looking at was the very bottom of the ship.

We rose slowly over the curve of the hull and then floated across the *Britannic*'s decks. I couldn't believe my eyes. Except for some pink coral and a healthy coating of barnacles, the railings looked perfect. So did the windows along the promenade deck.

As we traveled toward the stern, I felt my excitement rising. I was looking at an almost perfect clone of the *Titanic*. But instead of being broken in two as the *Titanic* is, the *Britannic* just kept on going. It was in one beautiful piece. It was as if the *Titanic* had been made whole again.

CHAPTER ONE

Ghost Liner

The Unsinkable Wreck of R.M.S. *Titanic*

July 14, 1986

Inside the cramped submarine, all I could hear was the steady pinging of the sonar and the regular breathing of the pilot and engineer. I crouched on my knees, my eyes glued to the tiny viewport. The pings speeded up — that meant the wreck was close — and I strained to see beyond the small cone of light that pierced the endless underwater night.

"Come right!" I was so excited I was almost shouting, even though the two others with me inside *Alvin* were so close I could touch them. "Bingo!"

Like a ghost from the ancient past, the bow of the Royal Mail Steamer *Titanic*, the greatest shipwreck of all time, materialized out my viewport. After years of questing, I had arrived at the ship's last resting place.

(Opposite) Our little submarine *Alvin* rests on the *Titanic*'s portside boat deck while the underwater robot *Jason Junior* explores the ship's B-deck promenade.
(Top) The rust-shrouded prow of the *Titanic*.
(Above) I shoot video through one of *Alvin*'s tiny viewports.

April 10, 1912, noon
Tugboats help the *Titanic* pull away from the Southampton pier.

April 14, 1912, 11:39 P.M.
As the liner enters an ice field, a large iceberg lies directly in its path.

April 14, 1912, 11:40 P.M.
The iceberg scrapes along the *Titanic*'s starboard side.

April 15, 1912, 1:40 A.M.
Two hours after the collision, the bow of the *Titanic* is underwater.

April 15, 1912, 2:17 A.M.
The *Titanic* breaks in two and the bow section begins its final plunge.

TITANIC

Effortlessly we rose up the side of that famous bow, now weeping great tears of rust, past the huge anchor and up over the rail. We were the first in more than seventy years to "walk" on the *Titanic*'s deck! The giant windlasses used for raising and lowering the anchor still trailed their massive links of chain, as if ready to lower away. I felt as though I had walked into a dream.

In 1912, the *Titanic* had set sail on her maiden voyage, the largest, most luxurious ship the world had ever seen. On board were many of the rich and famous of the day. Then, on the fifth night out — tragedy. An iceberg, seen too late. Too few lifeboats. Pandemonium, and over 1,500 dead out of the more than 2,200 people on board.

Now the sub sailed out over the well deck, following the angle of the fallen foremast up toward the liner's bridge. We paused at the crow's nest. On the fateful night, lookout Frederick Fleet had been on duty here. It was he who warned the bridge: "Iceberg right ahead." Fleet was one of the lucky ones. He made it into a lifeboat and to safety.

The pilot set *Alvin* gently down on the bridge, not far from the telemotor control — all that remained of the steering mechanism of the ship. It was here that First Officer William Murdoch, desperate to avoid the mountain of ice that lay in the *Titanic*'s

(Above) *Alvin* investigates the bow section of the *Titanic* wreck. The stern lies in the distance. (Below left) The telemotor control that once held the ship's wheel; (middle) the A-deck promenade; (right) a section of bow railing.

path, shouted to the helmsman, "Hard a-starboard!" Then Murdoch watched in excruciating agony as the huge ship slowly began to turn — but it was too late and the iceberg fatally grazed the liner's side. I thought of Captain E. J. Smith rushing from his cabin to be told the terrible news. Thirty minutes later, after learning how quickly water was pouring into the ship, he knew that the "unsinkable" *Titanic* was doomed.

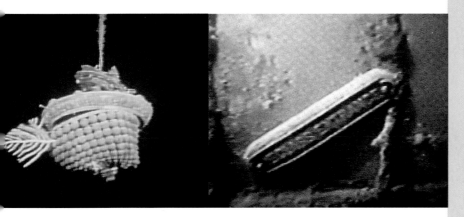

We lifted off from the bridge and headed toward the stern. Over a doorway we could make out the brass plate with the words: 1st Class Entrance. In my mind's eye I could see the deck surging with passengers as the crew tried to keep order during the loading of the lifeboats. The broken arm of a lifeboat davit hung over the side. From this spot port-side lifeboat No. 2 was launched — barely half full. Among the twenty-five people in a boat designed to carry more than forty were Minnie Coutts and her two boys, Willie and Neville. They were among the relatively few third-class passengers to survive the sinking.

As our tiny submarine continued toward the stern, we peered through the windows of first-class staterooms. The glass dome over the first-class grand staircase was long gone, providing a perfect opening for exploring the interior of the ship. But that would have to wait for a

(Opposite) *Jason Junior* explores the remains of the grand staircase and illuminates a light fixture from which a feathery sea pen has sprouted (above left). A brass plate (above right) still hangs over a first-class entrance door on the boat deck.

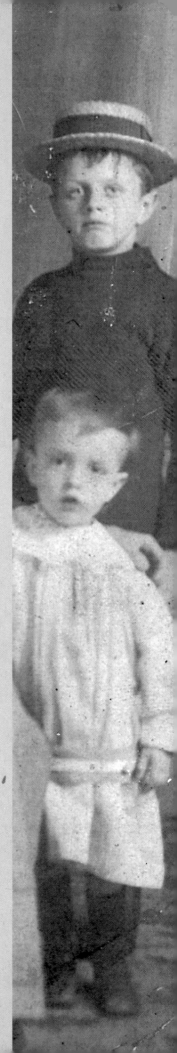

NEARLY LOST BECAUSE OF A HAT

Willie Coutts's hat nearly cost him his life. When the *Titanic* hit the iceberg, his mother Minnie roused eleven-year-old Willie and his baby brother Neville (right), got them dressed, and put on their lifebelts. Through the swirl of panicking passengers Minnie led her children out of third class toward what she hoped was safety. One officer handed his own lifebelt to Minnie, saying, "If the boat goes down you'll remember me." Another crewman led them to the boat deck. Minnie and Neville got in one of the last boats — but the officer in charge held Willie back. The rule was women and children first, and the hat Willie was wearing made him look too old. Willie's mother insisted but the officer refused again. Finally, good sense prevailed and Willie, too, stepped to safety.

TITANIC

later visit, when we would bring along our robotic "swimming eyeball," *Jason Junior*. As we continued back, I wondered what we would find. We already knew the ship lay in two pieces, with the stern nearly two thousand feet (six hundred meters) away. Suddenly the smooth steel sub-decking contorted into a tangle of twisted metal

where the stern had ripped free. Beyond it hundreds of objects that had spilled out when the ship broke in two were lying on the ocean floor.

As we floated out over this debris field, I found it hard to believe that only a thin film of sediment covered plates and bottles that had lain on the bottom for seventy-four years. One of the

HAUNTING MEMENTOS

Unlike its fairly intact bow section, the *Titanic*'s stern (left) literally blew apart on hitting the bottom. In the debris field between the bow and stern we saw hundreds of touching reminders of the tragedy. A porcelain doll's head (above right) is all that remains of an expensive French doll (inset). It may have belonged to Loraine Allison of Montreal (above left with her baby brother), the only child from first class who did not survive. A tin cup (below right) has come to rest near the round furnace door of one of the ship's huge boilers. (Below left) A brass lantern.

ship's boilers sat upright on the mud with a tin cup resting on it, as if set there by a human hand. Champagne bottles lay with their corks still intact. A porcelain doll's head stared at us from its final resting place in the soft ooze. Had it belonged to little Loraine Allison, the only child from first class who didn't survive that night? Most haunting of all

were the shoes and boots. Many of them lay in pairs where bodies had once fallen. Within a few weeks of the sinking, the corpses had been consumed by underwater creatures and their bones had been dissolved by the cold salt water. Only those shoes remain — mute reminders of the human cost of the *Titanic* tragedy.

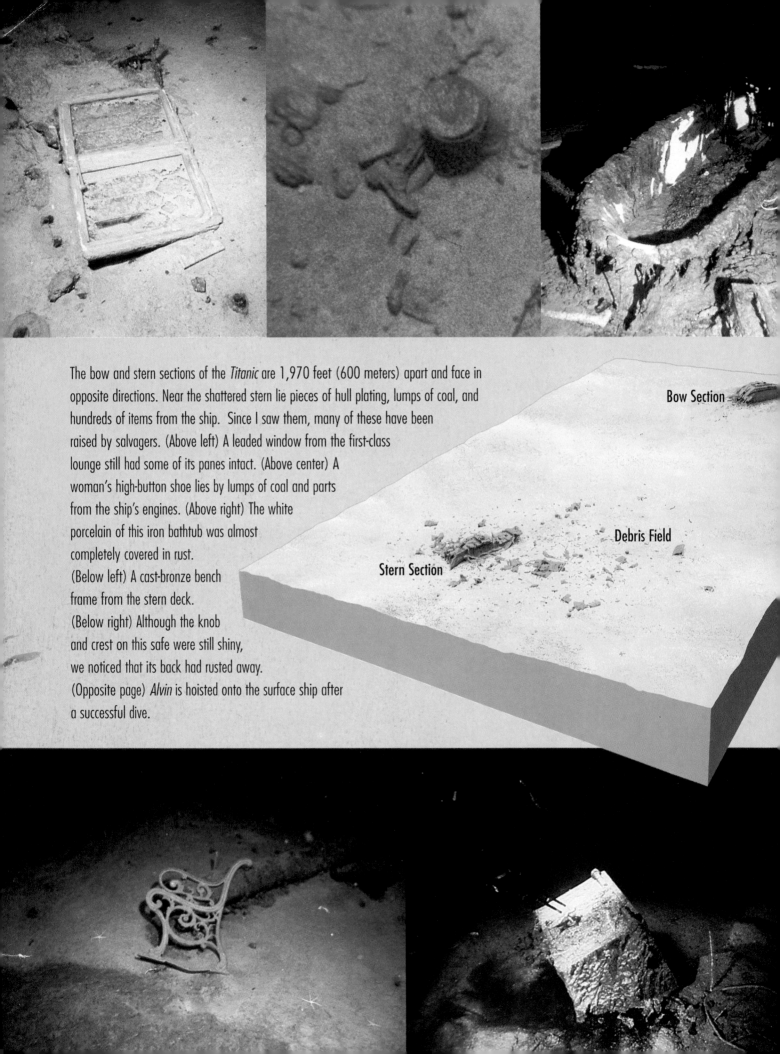

The bow and stern sections of the *Titanic* are 1,970 feet (600 meters) apart and face in opposite directions. Near the shattered stern lie pieces of hull plating, lumps of coal, and hundreds of items from the ship. Since I saw them, many of these have been raised by salvagers. (Above left) A leaded window from the first-class lounge still had some of its panes intact. (Above center) A woman's high-button shoe lies by lumps of coal and parts from the ship's engines. (Above right) The white porcelain of this iron bathtub was almost completely covered in rust.
(Below left) A cast-bronze bench frame from the stern deck.
(Below right) Although the knob and crest on this safe were still shiny, we noticed that its back had rusted away.
(Opposite page) *Alvin* is hoisted onto the surface ship after a successful dive.

Bow Section

Debris Field

Stern Section

TITANIC

After only two hours on the bottom, it was time for *Alvin* to begin the long ascent back to the surface ship, two and a half miles (four kilometers) above. As we headed back to the surface, I was already impatient to return to the *Titanic*. We had only begun to plumb its secrets.

As the sub rose silently through the blackness, we turned on the stereo and relaxed, but the images from this first dive kept coming back. I kept seeing those empty davits and thinking of all the people swimming in the icy Atlantic after the ship went down. I imagined Willie Coutts, huddled in his lifeboat, hearing the desperate chorus of cries for help and wondering why the adults didn't go back until it was too late.

The wreck we had discovered in 1985 had already caused a sensation around the world. I knew that unlike most media events, the excitement about the discovery of the *Titanic* was more than just a passing fad. People had been fascinated by the *Titanic* story — the first great modern disaster — long before the wreck was found. But I had no idea that the *Titanic* was only the most famous of the transatlantic liners that had disappeared beneath the sea.

CHAPTER TWO

Fourteen Minutes of Terror

The Tragedy of the *Empress of Ireland*

May 29, 1914

Only two years after the *Titanic* sank, there was another terrible shipwreck, this one in the St. Lawrence River east of Quebec City. On the early morning of May 29, 1914, a Norwegian coal ship called the *Storstad* rammed the Canadian Pacific passenger ship *Empress of Ireland* in thick fog. The *Empress* sank in only fourteen minutes with a terrible loss of life.

It takes a modern scuba diver only a minute or two to descend the 130 feet (40 meters) to the wreck of the *Empress of Ireland*. But only very experienced divers consider going down. Because of the depth and the intense cold, divers can spend no more than an hour inside the wreck before returning to the surface. On the way back, they have to pause for as long as two hours to allow the dissolved gases in the blood to release slowly. Otherwise, a gas bubble will form in the veins, causing acute pain (the bends) or even death. Not a trip to be taken lightly.

An hour isn't much time to explore a ghostly giant more than five hundred feet (150 meters) long, that lies in almost total darkness. Although some daylight makes it

(Above) The *Empress of Ireland* was one of the two largest and fastest ships on the run between Liverpool and Quebec City. Although smaller, slower, and less opulent than the *Titanic,* the *Empress* was still a very fine liner, with elegant public rooms for the first-class passengers and a five-piece string orchestra to serenade them at dinner. When fully booked, it could carry approximately 1,550 passengers—300 in first class, 450 in second and 800 in third.

down to the wreck, it's a dim twilight from which all the color has been filtered out. And once inside the wreck, it's always nighttime.

The diving conditions are unpredictable and dangerous. Even in summer, the St. Lawrence River east of Rimouski, Quebec, is barely warmer than freezing and the tidal currents run up to five knots. For safety, divers follow a long rope down to the ship.

Getting inside the *Empress of Ireland* is easier than with most wrecks, however, because the ship's owners, Canadian Pacific, blasted a hole into the hull a few weeks after the disaster to recover $150,000 worth of silver bullion — worth about two million today — and the all-important mail going from Canada to England. That hole is the diver's entrance into what was once the elegant first-class dining room.

As you go deeper inside the ship, you can easily get lost in the black tunnels and twisted caverns that were once well-lit corridors and airy public rooms. The ship lies at a sharp angle, and

EMPRESS OF IRELAND

silt carried by the river has built up over the more than eighty years since the *Empress* sank. The right side of every room is buried in it and everything — from pieces of furniture to pots and pans from the first-class kitchen — juts out of the mud. Each time you visit the ship, the sediment has shifted; often a familiar landmark has disappeared. One diver I know, who has been down to the *Empress* many times, remembers discovering a whole box of neatly bundled newspapers sticking out of the sediment in the mail room. The paper was still white, the newsprint still readable, including the date — May 27, 1914, one day before the ship left port. The next time he visited, the newspapers

were gone, buried by the shifting mud.

But the place no diver ever forgets is what some call "the boneyard," the stewards' dormitory where the broken skeletons of the sixty stewards who slept there are jumbled together in a ghastly heap. The reason human bones have survived on the *Empress* and not on the *Titanic* wreck is unclear since both sank in salt water. It may have something to do with the *Titanic's* far greater depth.

Of all the ghost liners, the *Empress of Ireland* has one of the most terrifying stories to tell. For most of the more than a thousand passengers asleep in their cabins, death came

quickly. One minute they were breathing air, the next they were sucking in ice-cold water. Few had time to even shout or grab for a lifebelt. But some, mostly those in the higher-up first-class cabins, made it out onto the deck and into the lifeboats.

Within minutes of the collision, however, the *Empress of Ireland* had listed so far on its right side that it became impossible to launch any more boats. Ten or eleven minutes after the collision, the ship lurched violently over on its side, throwing hundreds of people into the near-freezing water. The ship's commander, Captain Henry Kendall, was catapulted from his perch on one side of the bridge. But at least seven hundred men, women, and children managed to hold on. As the liner rolled over, they struggled over the rail and onto the side of the ship's hull. For a minute or two it seemed as if the *Empress* had run aground and they were safe. "It was just like sitting on the beach watching the tide come in," remembered one passenger. "The waves came splashing up the slope of steel, and then retired one after another. But each came a little higher than the last."

Fourteen minutes after being struck, the *Empress*'s stern rose briefly out of the water, then its hull sank out of sight. Shrieks and wails filled the air as those in the water drowned or died of hypothermia.

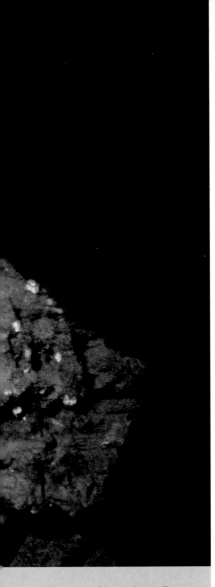

(Above) A lifeboat that still rests on the liner's deck. Because the *Empress* sank so quickly after being rammed, many of its lifeboats were never launched.
(Below) A set of stairs on board the ship.

(Top) Passengers relax in the music room. (Middle) Captain Henry Kendall strolls the deck with one of his passengers. (Above) The first-class dining saloon. (Below) Deck cricket being played on the promenade deck.

The lucky ones were hauled shivering, some half-dead, into the few lifeboats there had been time to launch earlier.

One of them was Captain Kendall. After being thrown from the bridge, Captain Kendall had sunk so deep that by the time he resurfaced, the *Empress* was gone. He clung to a wooden grating long enough for a nearby lifeboat to pull him out of the water.

Immediately, he took command of rescue operations. Once his own boat was full to the point of sinking, he ordered the crewmen to pull toward the lights of the mysterious vessel that had rammed them. The fog had been so dense that Kendall had only seen this other ship a few moments before it struck his own, and he still didn't know its name or nationality.

Captain Kendall led several trips to rescue

(Top) The *Empress* begins its final plunge. (Below left) Passengers cling to the side of the capsized ship. (Below right) These Salvation Army band members were traveling to a big convention in London, England. All of them perished. (Opposite) An illustration from a French magazine shows lifeboats searching the wreckage for survivors.

survivors. Only when there was no hope of finding anyone else alive, did he return to the other ship for good. He learned that its name was the *Storstad* and that it was a Norwegian coal carrier. As the May dawn broke, he confronted the *Storstad*'s captain. "You have sunk my ship," he accused the Norwegian. And so he would believe until his dying day.

APRÈS LA CATASTROPHE DE L' "EMPRESS-OF-IRELAND"
La recherche des victimes

Where the *Empress* now lies on the cold, dim riverbed, the modern diver will find no evidence to settle the question of who is to blame for the collision that sank the *Empress of Ireland* and sent more than a thousand people to their deaths.

Captain Kendall swore that he had clearly altered course before the fog moved in, a maneuver that should have been clearly seen and understood by those on the *Storstad*. Once in the fog, he reversed his engines to bring the ship to a stop, blowing his whistle to signal this, and taking care to hold the *Empress* exactly on course.

The men on the *Storstad* claimed they had seen the *Empress* turn back toward shore just before the fog enveloped their ship. In response, they had turned right to avoid her. But in reality, they had turned directly into her. They vowed they never heard the whistle blasts signaling Captain Kendall's decision to stop his ship and wait out the fog.

If there is no clue as to who was to blame, divers can easily discover why the *Empress* sank so quickly. The *Storstad*'s bow punctured only two of the *Empress*'s watertight compartments, and the ship's builders had designed it to stay afloat with exactly this much damage. But as divers swim along the port side of the hull, they can see that many of the portholes are open. These portholes were not flung open by the impact with the bottom.

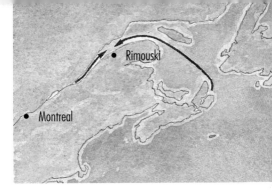

The *Empress of Ireland* and the *Storstad* sight each other near Rimouski, Quebec.

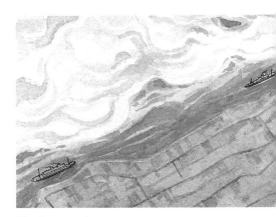

The *Empress* alters course to port just as the fog rolls in.

When the *Storstad* emerges from the fog, Captain Kendall orders a starboard turn.

The *Storstad*'s bow crashes into the starboard side of the *Empress*'s hull.

GRACE HANAGAN'S LUCK

When the *Empress of Ireland* began to turn over, seven-year-old Grace Hanagan (above) and her parents were perched on the high side of the railing. Then the ship lurched, and all three were thrown into the water. Grace went under twice but managed to grab a piece of wreckage. Soon she drifted away from her parents. When she saw a lifeboat, she called out for help. The boat was full, but the passengers lifted her to safety and squeezed her in. The next thing she remembered was waking up in a bed on the *Storstad*. Later, she learned that both her parents had died in the water.

They had been left open by passengers who craved some fresh air in the cramped and poorly ventilated staterooms. This was against the rules. Once a ship was under way, the operating instructions required all portholes to be closed. But it was a rule frequently broken, especially in sheltered waters such as those of the St. Lawrence.

When the *Empress* began its rapid tilt to starboard, water soon began to pour through the lowest portholes, usually only five feet (one and a half meters) above the waterline. Once those portholes went under, the *Empress*'s end was inevitable. Water quickly flooded into parts of the ship that had not been damaged by the *Storstad*'s bow.

Of the 1,477 on board, 1,012 died, 840 of them passengers. This was eight more passengers than had died on the *Titanic*. Yet the *Empress of Ireland* never gained anything like the *Titanic*'s fame. It wasn't as big or as fashionable a ship — and had never claimed to be unsinkable. Only a few months after the *Empress of Ireland* sank, the First World War broke out, and the newspapers had other tragedies to report. Today, the ghostly wreck is the most powerful reminder of this great but almost forgotten maritime disaster.

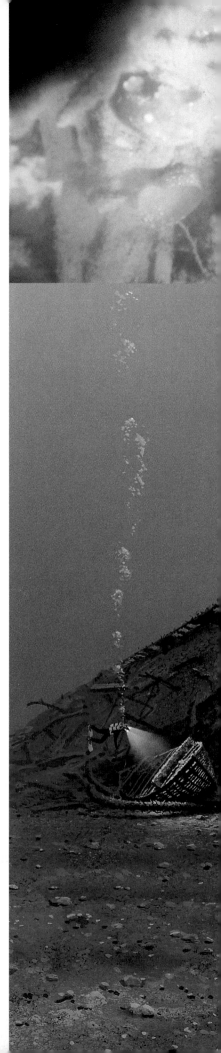

In the icy cold of the St. Lawrence River, the wreck of the *Empress* (below) lies at a depth of 130 feet (40 meters). But dangerous currents and limited visibility make it a challenge even for experienced divers. (Left) A human skull amidst the wreckage. (Right) The pattern of some floor tiles shows through the sediment.

CHAPTER THREE

Casualty of War:

The Sinking of the *Lusitania*

May 7, 1915

I t was a lovely afternoon for a spring picnic, and the Henderson family was taking full advantage of the fine weather. For six-year-old George, the family's favorite picnic spot had an extra-special allure. The Old Head of Kinsale, not very far from his home in Bandon on the south coast of Ireland, commanded a panoramic view of one of the busiest British sea-lanes. This was the route followed by the enormous passenger ships that traveled between North America and England.

After lunch, George and his twin older brothers played soccer on the grass while their parents lounged nearby. A shout from their father interrupted their game. A ship coming from the west — across the Atlantic — was just rounding Point McSherry, a little over twelve miles (nineteen kilometers) away. He called them to come and look.

Young George had never seen anything so big in his life: "Four massive funnels, three of them smoking away merrily." The Henderson family watched in fascination as the bright sunlight played on the white superstructure and the black funnels and danced on the blue sea. There was an almost joyful quality to the scene that made it hard to believe Great Britain was at war.

As George watched, a giant fountain of water and smoke shot up just beyond the ship. The vessel "stuttered," but kept on going. For a few moments the fountain seemed frozen in mid-air. As it collapsed, the sound of an explosion reached the picnickers. It reminded George of a distant rifle shot. Then came a second explosion at least as loud as the first. The ship now seemed to be turning toward them.

KEN MARSCHALL

(Left) The *Lusitania* leaves the Cunard pier in New York as she begins her final voyage.
(Below left) The German warning that appeared in U.S. newspapers on the morning of the ship's departure.
(Below right) The *Lusitania*'s final moments.

OCEAN TRAVEL.

NOTICE!

TRAVELLERS intending to embark on the Atlantic voyage are reminded that a state of war exists between Germany and her allies and GreatBritian and her allies; that the zone of war includes the waters adjacent to the British Isles; that, in accordance with formal notice given by the Imperial German Government, vessels flying the flag of Great Britian, or of any of her allies, are liable to destruction in those waters and that travellers sailing in the war zone on ships of Great Britian or her allies do so at their own risk.

IMPERIAL GERMAN EMBASSY,
WASHINGTON, D. C., APRIL 22, 1915.

OCEAN TRAVEL

CUNARD

EUROPE VIA LIVERPOOL

LUSITANIA

Fastest and Largest Steamer now in Atlantic Service Sails

SATURDAY, MAY 1, 10 A. M.

Transylvania - Fri. May 7, 5 P.M.
Orduna - Tues. May 18, 10 A.M.
Tuscania - Fri. May 21, 5 P.M.
LUSITANIA - Sat. May 29, 10 A.M.
Transylvania - Fri., June 4, 5 P.M.
Gibraltar—Genoa—Naples—Piraeus
S.S. Carpathia, Thur., May 13, Noon

ROUND THE WORLD TOURS
Through bookings to all principal Ports
of the World
Company's Office, 21-24 State St., N. Y.

G eorge Henderson had just witnessed the beginning of the end of R.M.S. *Lusitania*, one of the two fastest ships in the world. The cause of the first explosion was a torpedo from a German submarine. The cause of the second remains a mystery. The *Lusitania* had turned toward shore because its captain was desperately trying to beach his ship before it sank.

Some of the passengers who suddenly found themselves scrambling for the lifeboats may have known they were taking a calculated risk when they had boarded the *Lusitania* in New York. That same day, the German embassy had placed an announcement in the New York newspapers warning that "vessels flying the flag of Great Britain, or any of her allies, are liable to destruction." At this time, the United States was not at war with Germany. But any American traveling on the *Lusitania* could be in danger. It was a British ship and, from the German point of view, fair game. Few passengers, if any, took the warnings seriously, however. They couldn't believe a German submarine would sink an unarmed passenger ship. And such was the fame of the *Lusitania*, and of her sister ship, the *Mauretania*, that it seemed inconceivable she could be sunk. These two celebrated luxury liners, the pride of the Cunard Line, had entered service in 1907 and broken transatlantic speed records the same year. Their immediate success had spurred the White Star Line to build its equally famous liners — the *Olympic* and the *Titanic*. Now, like the *Titanic*, another transatlantic superstar was about to meet a tragic end.

George Henderson and his family watched as the ship's bow began to sink steadily beneath the water. As the bow dipped, the stern rose until George could see one of its propellers spinning slowly in the air. Some lifeboats were pulling away from the ship. Others had tipped on launching or dropped on top of other boats. Many people splashed about in the sea. For a moment, when the ship was at about a forty-five degree angle, it seemed to hang there, suspended. Then, ever so slowly, almost gracefully, it slid beneath the waves, leaving the sea boiling. George still didn't know the vessel's name, only that one minute it was sailing along and a few minutes later it was gone.

LUSITANIA

Eighteen minutes after the initial explosion, the *Lusitania* began its final plunge. It had lasted only four minutes longer than the *Empress of Ireland*. The ship took with it all but 764 of the 1,959 people on board. Only a few hundred managed to scramble into the handful of lifeboats that were launched. Many more drowned in the water because they hadn't had time to put on a lifebelt.

But the crucial statistic was the number of Americans who died when the *Lusitania* sank, 123 of the 189 on board. The United States government expressed outrage at Germany's sinking of a passenger ship, and the horrifying loss of life helped turn American public opinion in favor of entering the war on the British side.

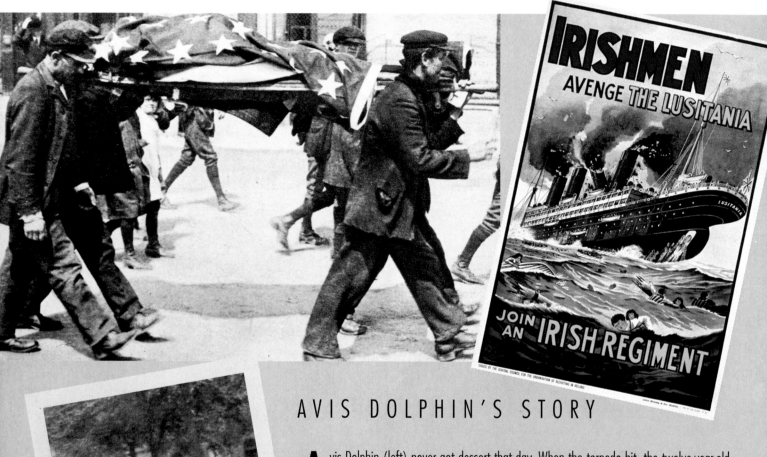

AVIS DOLPHIN'S STORY

Avis Dolphin (left) never got dessert that day. When the torpedo hit, the twelve-year-old and her two friends, Sarah and Hilda, were finishing lunch in the *Lusitania*'s second-class dining room. A second explosion sent waiters sprawling and plates and cutlery flying. Panic ensued, but luckily, Ian Holbourn, a kindly gentleman Avis had befriended earlier in the voyage, guided the three girls from the dining room. In his cabin, Holbourn found them life jackets and then saw all three girls to a lifeboat. Unfortunately, as it was being lowered, two men leaped into it from the deck, flipping it. Avis survived — as did Ian Holbourn — but Hilda and Sarah were among the 1,195 who died. (Above left) Many bodies were brought ashore at Queenstown, Ireland. (Above right) British anger over the sinking is shown in this recruiting poster. (Opposite) Seventy-eight years later, our submersible *Delta* visits the scene of the tragedy.

In August 1993, when I led an expedition to explore the wreck of the *Lusitania*, no one had yet solved the mystery that has puzzled historians since the day it sank: what caused the second explosion that followed so soon after the torpedo detonated? We know from the submarine captain's own log that he fired one — and only one — torpedo at the ship. Yet we also know from many eyewitness accounts that there were two explosions, not one; in fact, many survivors claimed that the second explosion was more violent than the first.

Some historians have argued that the *Lusitania* carried a secret cargo of munitions that was detonated by the torpedo explosion. Conspiracy theorists have even suggested that

LUSITANIA

Sir Winston Churchill, the First Sea Lord in charge of the British navy, deliberately let the Germans discover where the *Lusitania* would sail so that they would sink her and force the Americans to enter the war. But no one had ever brought forward any convincing proof to support any of these theories.

Nonetheless, we hoped there would be enough clues on the ocean floor to settle the question. As we expected, the *Lusitania* wreck was in terrible shape. The Irish navy seems to have used it for target practice, judging from the holes in the hull and the unexploded depth charges on the bottom — which made our exploration even more dangerous than usual. Parts of the ship were draped in a deadly tangle of fishing nets.

Despite these hazards, we were able to examine the hull area outside the hold, located deep down in the ship's hull, where any explosives would have been stored. We found no evidence that an explosion had originated there.

In the end we had to conclude that the only solid clues to the mystery lay scattered on the seabed near the ship: lumps of coal that had once been inside the hull. It seems likely that when the torpedo hit, it ripped open one of the *Lusitania*'s coal bunkers. Near the end of an Atlantic crossing these would have been almost empty. The explosion would have kicked up a lot of coal dust, however, and coal dust, when mixed with oxygen, is as explosive as dynamite. One

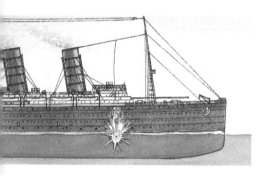

The torpedo strikes the *Lusitania*'s hull on the starboard side at a point just below the bridge.

In the empty starboard coal bunkers, coal dust is stirred up by the torpedo's impact.

The mixture of coal dust and oxygen ignites, setting off a powerful explosion that rips a gaping hole in the hull. The *Lusitania* is now doomed.

(Above) *Delta* shines its light on the starboard anchor, still hanging from its place on the bow. Snagged fishing nets float over the wreck. (Right) Through the rust, an embossed letter A from the ship's name can just be made out.
(Far right) The telegraph from the stern docking bridge.

spark from the initial explosion would have been enough to detonate this coal and oxygen mixture. I believe it was the force of this second explosion, far more damaging than the torpedo itself, that caused the ship to sink.

After the sinking of the *Lusitania*, George Henderson's family continued to come for picnics on the same bluff overlooking the Celtic Sea, but they never saw another ship go down. Many years later, when George had a grandchild the same age as he was when the *Lusitania* sank, he remembered the day clearly: "Although time fades and the little gray cells get worn out," he said, "I can still sit here now and see that liner . . . just sliding beneath the waves."

(Far left) I stand next to one of the *Lusitania*'s propellers, previously salvaged from the wreck. (Left) One of the *Lusitania*'s unusual hinge-topped vents. (Right) A bathtub, its shower intact, rests beside a skylight. (Far right) The remains of a woman's shoe. (Below) *Delta* explores the stern, while the robot vehicle *Jason* investigates forward.

CHAPTER FOUR

Innocent Victim:
The Loss of H.M.H.S. *Britannic*

November 21, 1916

When we arrived at the wreck of the *Britannic* in late August 1995, we were only the second team to visit the site since the ship sank in November 1916. The first expedition, led by famous French oceanographer Jacques Cousteau, had explored the wreck in 1976. But Cousteau had come back with an incomplete notion of the state of the ship — his underwater cameras just weren't good enough. Exactly what sank the *Britannic* — a mine or a torpedo — remained uncertain. We hoped we would find something to settle the debate. One thing was sure, however: the *Britannic* had been sailing through dangerous waters. Only a little more than a year had passed since the sinking of the *Lusitania*, and German submarines continued to take a terrible toll on British shipping in the Atlantic and here, in the Mediterranean.

As a hospital ship, the *Britannic* was theoretically immune from enemy attack. She was painted white, with big red crosses on her sides and superstructure, so that no enemy vessel would mistake her for a combatant. But German submarines didn't always respect these rules. And underwater mines don't distinguish between friend and foe.

I was interested in settling the question of what sank the *Britannic*, but the most exciting thing about visiting the wreck was the chance to get to know the *Titanic*'s younger sister. The *Britannic* had been built to be even more splendid than either the *Olympic* or the *Titanic*.

The *Gigantic*, to use its original name, would have boasted the most luxurious trappings of any White Star liner, including a pipe organ on the landing of the grand staircase. It was eighteen inches (half a meter) wider than its predecessors because of an inner watertight skin designed to make it even safer. The watertight bulkheads rose higher to prevent what

(Opposite) The *Britannic* wearing the colors of a hospital ship. (Top) A White Star booklet commemorated *Britannic*'s launch on February 26, 1914. (Above) Before the *Titanic* sank, White Star planned to name its third huge liner *Gigantic*.

The *Britannic* was intended to be the largest, most luxurious — and safest — ship flying the British flag. This drawing of the reception room (above) next to the first-class restaurant shows that its interiors would have been even more splendid than the *Titanic*'s. The grand staircase (left) was to be made even grander by the addition of a huge pipe organ (right). But with the outbreak of World War I, the *Britannic* became a hospital ship. Luxurious paneling and elaborate fittings were taken out and the first-class dining room became an intensive-care ward.

BRITANNIC

happened when the *Titanic* sank — as the *Titanic*'s bow dipped lower, water spilled over the bulkheads, filling one compartment after another. *Britannic* had more than enough lifeboats for all its passengers and crew. To launch them, she was equipped with huge davits that could swing a boat right over to the opposite side of the ship if necessary. In fact, its builders had designed the ship to survive the kind of collision that sank the *Titanic* — and that was about the worst accident anyone could imagine.

November 21, 1916, was a glorious sunny morning, and James Vickers was glad to be alive. But the fifteen-year-old Sea Scout felt the same excitement every time the *Britannic* entered a war zone. One of sixteen teenage boys on the great hospital ship, he would soon be kept busy helping the orderlies to carry the wounded on board when they arrived at Mudros in the eastern Mediterranean later that day. In the meantime, however, he stood on the ship's bridge, ready to carry out his other work as captain's messenger, a job that gave him the run of the giant vessel.

A year earlier, the liner *Britannic* had been nearly ready to enter passenger service. The huge boilers and engines were in place, the miles of plumbing and electrical wiring were complete. Workmen had begun installing the fancy paneling and the other expensive appointments in the first-class passenger areas. Then the call had come from the British Admiralty: the *Titanic*'s younger sister had been requisitioned as a hospital ship.

In the weeks that followed, all the fancy fittings were removed and placed in storage, and the equipment needed for a floating hospital was brought on board. Soon the promenade decks were lined with cots and the first-class dining room had become the intensive-care ward. There the most seriously wounded would stay before and after surgery in the operating theater next door — formerly the grand reception room. Most of the wounded would sleep in the public rooms on the upper decks — close to the lifeboats in case the call came to abandon ship. The first-class staterooms served as quarters for the doctors, the nursing supervisor, the medical corps officers, and the chaplains. The lesser nurses and orderlies, including the Sea Scouts, made do with cabins originally intended for the lower

(Top) Two nurses stand in one of the enclosed promenade decks that has been converted into a hospital ward. (Above) The *Britannic* as it looked in November of 1916, showing the wear of its wartime service. (Below) A group photograph shows the Sea Scouts from the *Britannic*. Young scouts served on many non-combat ships during the First World War.

classes. Not that James or any of his fellow scouts were complaining about their quarters. To them the *Britannic* was a marvel.

As eight o'clock, the hour for breakfast, passed, James noticed how hungry he was. Most of his fellow scouts, who worked for other

ship's officers or operated the elevators that had been built to carry the ship's passengers would be sitting down to eat right now. Properly, he should have stayed on the bridge. But as the captain and his officers seemed completely absorbed with navigating the *Britannic* through the channel between the islands of Kea and Makronisos, just off the Greek mainland, he thought he might slip away. About ten minutes past eight, he decided to approach the captain. If there was nothing to do, he might as well head for the dining room.

Just as James started to walk forward, he felt a bump and the ship "sort of shivered from end to end." It was as if the *Britannic* had collided with something, but the Aegean Sea was clear of vessels. James had to struggle to keep from losing his balance. He heard someone shout — probably one of the officers — and then crewmen began to run out onto the deck below. The captain had already sounded an alarm. But James couldn't see any sign of a submarine. What could possibly have happened?

"My heart was in my mouth," the young man later remembered, "but when I saw the captain standing there, cool and quiet, I thought to myself, 'It's all right,' and I felt a deal more comfortable, and I went to the locker and got out the captain's megaphone according to orders, and I stood alongside the captain on the bridge to see if he had any orders for me."

Captain Charles Bartlett made a desperate gamble. Seeing the island of Kea not far away, he steered the ship toward it at top speed. He hoped he could beach her. Instead, the *Britannic* began flooding even faster, and he quickly ordered the ship stopped. Before he did, however, two boats had been launched without permission. They

were sucked into the still-turning propellers and smashed to kindling. Thirty people were killed and another forty were injured.

James stayed at his post until almost all the lifeboats had left. Then Captain Bartlett ordered him to abandon ship. He watched the great liner's final moments from an overcrowded lifeboat. "I saw the *Britannic* sink," he remembered. "She went down bow first, and the propellers came high out of the water, and I felt pretty flabbergasted. As we were rowing along, we saw a raft with a man standing on it,

and a boat went up to it and raised a cheer, and
we saw it was Captain Bartlett, and we cheered
too." The captain had calmly walked off the
starboard wing of the bridge as the ship sank,
then had swum to a collapsible lifeboat. Now
he took charge of the rescue.

Only fifty-five minutes had passed between
the explosion and the sinking. *Britannic* was
supposed to be the safest ship afloat, able to
survive a catastrophe as bad as that which had
sunk the *Titanic*. But the *Titanic* had taken
more than two hours to sink. *Britannic*'s

designers had never dreamed she'd fall victim
to a mine or torpedo, and her safety features
weren't much good against them. And, as
with the *Empress of Ireland*, hundreds of
portholes had been left open, against orders.
That speeded up the flooding.

Thirty-five lifeboats and many swimmers
dotted the calm, warm Mediterranean under a
brilliant blue sky. After only a few minutes had
passed, the first distant plume of smoke from a
ship's stack appeared on the horizon. Help was
on the way.

(Above) The U.S. Navy's nuclear-powered *NR-1* prepares for another dive to the wreck. (Below) Two of the *Olympic*'s three huge propellers, identical to the *Britannic*'s, dwarf shipyard workers during construction. (Right) A ghostly propeller viewed from the stern of the wreck.

'll never forget the moment when *Voyager*, one of our remotely operated vehicles, first came in close on one of the *Britannic*'s propellers. Seen in three dimensions, the huge blades of the propeller seemed to fill the room. I suddenly felt very small. The incredible size and power of the *Britannic* and the *Titanic* became even more real to me.

It turned out that the *Britannic* was in even better shape than I'd dared hope. Yes, she was encrusted with a thin layer of barnacles and coral, but the hull and upper decks were amazingly well preserved. The outer covering that protected the dome over the grand staircase remained intact — most of the panes of glass

were still in place! The railings and items of deck hardware looked only in need of a wire brush to return them to an almost pristine state. And one set of huge gantry davits still towered above the deck, swung out as if they were about to launch a lifeboat. More amazing still, we found all four of the ship's funnels in the debris field near the ship, the first time in my experience these fragile cylinders of steel have remained in one piece at a wreck site.

But there's no question the biggest highlight for me was seeing the whole ship in one piece, completely recognizable. Except for the rent in the bow, it seemed only to need a good scrubbing to be ready to set out to sea again. For

years I'd held in my mind's eye a torn picture of the *Titanic* — the beautifully preserved bow, the mangled stern. Now it was as if the stern had magically been repaired and the two pieces of the picture joined together again.

So, was it a mine or a torpedo that sank the *Britannic?* With only a few hours left before we had to pack up our ROVs and head home, we set off in search of the anchors that would have been used to tether floating mines in place. These would be powerful circumstantial evidence that a mine sank the ship. But without any clear debris trail — and with only those four fallen funnels — we couldn't be sure how the ship drifted before it went down. We searched the surrounding area for several hours, but found nothing. And so the debate remains unresolved. What sank the *Britannic?* You take your pick. Was it a mine, as seems most likely? Or was it a torpedo, as many of those on the ship believed?

By the end of our week exploring the wreck, I was convinced that I had finally found the perfect ship to fulfill a long-held dream. Here was the ideal site for the first-ever underwater museum.

If my dream comes true, some day you'll be able to visit the *Britannic* without going to Greece. You'll only need to visit a website connected to the *Britannic* satellite network. Underwater cameras permanently mounted on the wreck — and inside it — will beam back pictures. Visitors will be able to guide these camera robots into places we could only imagine during our brief visit. We have the technology. Now all we need is the money and the will.

On the morning of Tuesday, November 21, 1916, the *Britannic* entered a narrow channel between the islands of Kea and Makronisos off the coast of Greece.

At 8:12 A.M., the ship probably struck a single mine, which blasted a hole in the starboard side of the hull near the bow.

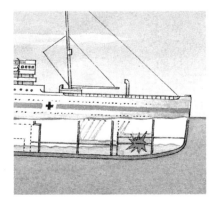

Within minutes the ship was down at the bow and leaning far enough to starboard for water to pour in through the open portholes.

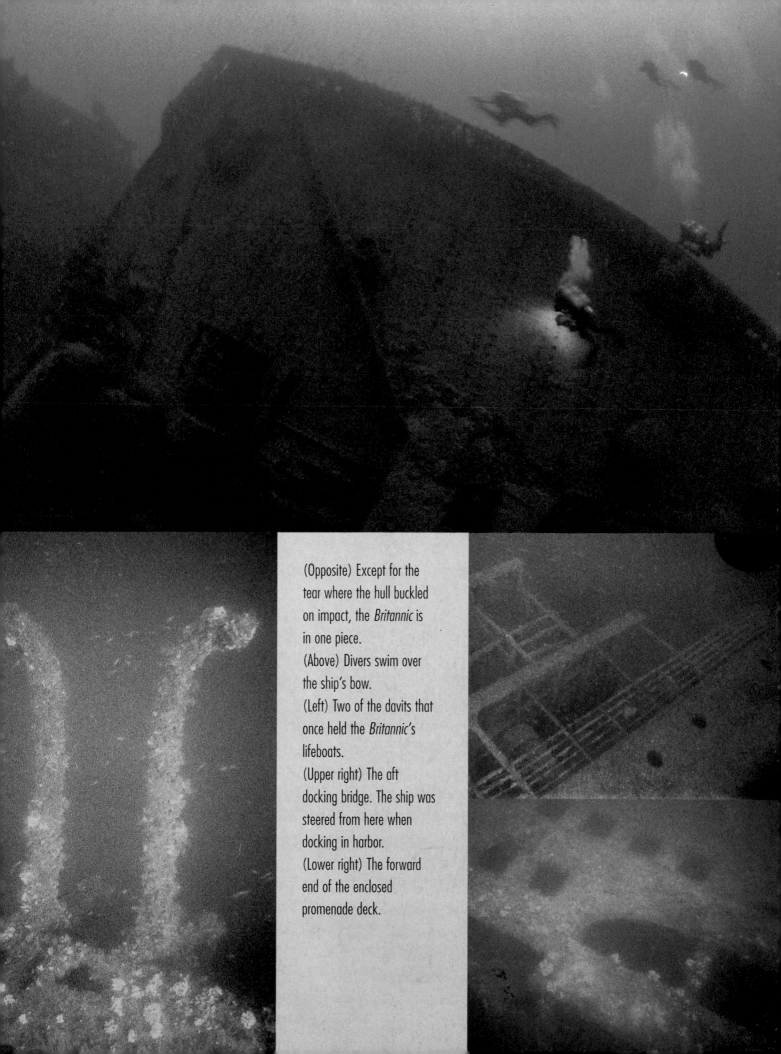

(Opposite) Except for the tear where the hull buckled on impact, the *Britannic* is in one piece.

(Above) Divers swim over the ship's bow.

(Left) Two of the davits that once held the *Britannic*'s lifeboats.

(Upper right) The aft docking bridge. The ship was steered from here when docking in harbor.

(Lower right) The forward end of the enclosed promenade deck.

CHAPTER FIVE

Amazing Rescue

The Collision of the *Stockholm* and the *Andrea Doria*

July 25, 1956

Nearly four decades would pass after the *Britannic* sank before tragedy again struck one of the great transatlantic ocean liners in peacetime. The circumstances were uncannily similar to those that led to the sinking of the *Empress of Ireland*, but the Italian luxury liner *Andrea Doria* was equipped with a safety feature that would have easily saved even the *Titanic*: radar. What's more, as the first passenger ship built in Italy following the Second World War, the *Andrea Doria* was supposed to be one of the safest ships afloat.

(Top) The *Andrea Doria* at anchor flying all her flags.

(Above left) The bow deck and bridge of the *Cristoforo Colombo*, the nearly identical twin of the *Andrea Doria*. (Above center) Three weeks before the sinking, the *Andrea Doria* prepares to depart from New York for the last time. (Above right) The Manhattan skyline as seen from the bow of the *Andrea Doria*.

Linda Morgan could hardly contain her excitement. The voyage from Italy was almost over. Tomorrow the ship would arrive in New York and she would be reunited with her father, whom she hadn't seen in over a year. And tonight, she and her little sister Joan were dining with the captain!

Linda was fourteen. Linda's mom was divorced from her real dad, Edward P. Morgan, who was a famous broadcaster for ABC Radio and lived in New York. She now lived in Spain with her mother Jane, her eight-year-old half-sister Joan, and her stepfather Camille Cianfarra, the Madrid correspondent for the *New York Times*. At home she spoke more Spanish than English. She loved her stepfather, but she missed her dad.

Mr. and Mrs. Cianfarra and their daughters dressed in their fanciest clothes for the last dinner of the voyage from Genoa to New York. They had spent more than a week on this wonderful ship, long enough to feel at ease on the *Andrea Doria*. Linda no longer noticed the constant rise and fall as the ship's hull, almost seven hundred feet (220 meters) long, rode gently on the ocean swells.

The *Andrea Doria*, named after a famous sixteenth-century Genoese admiral, was like a fancy resort hotel. There were beautiful paintings on the walls, and a giant bronze statue of Admiral Andrea Doria in the first-class

ANDREA DORIA

lounge. There were game rooms and exercise rooms and, best of all, three outdoor swimming pools. The weather had been hot and sunny most of the trip, and Linda and her sister had spent many happy hours splashing in the first-class pool.

When Linda and her family left their cabins to walk to dinner, she carried with her a slender, red hardcover book. This was her Camp Fire Girls autograph book in which she had collected the signatures of famous movie stars such as Gregory Peck and Cary Grant, and of famous writers such as John Steinbeck. Being the daughter and stepdaughter of journalists meant that Linda had already met a lot of important people. Tonight she planned to add Captain Piero Calamai's name to her collection.

But when the Cianfarras arrived at the captain's table, the steward politely informed them that Captain Calamai would not be joining them that evening. For some hours the *Andrea Doria* had been steaming through fog. The ship was now entering some of the busiest shipping lanes in the

The *Andrea Doria* was like a luxurious resort hotel. (Above left) The first-class pool was one of three on board.(Top right) A game of deck tennis. (Above right) Relaxing in a second-class cabin. (Far right) The bunkbeds in third-class cabins were popular with children.(Below) The *Andrea Doria's* captain, Piero Calamai.

world, the approach to New York harbor. His duty was to remain on the bridge.

While the Cianfarras dug into the many courses of delicious Italian food from the ship's kitchen, the scene on the *Andrea Doria*'s bridge was one of quiet professionalism. As a veteran of thirty-nine years at sea and hundreds of Atlantic crossings, Captain Calamai was the perfect man to command the Italian Line's flagship. He didn't take unnecessary risks, but neither did he stick strictly to the book. As a seasoned mariner, he would stretch the rules when he thought it justified. That's exactly what the *Titanic*'s Captain Smith had been doing when he continued sailing at full speed despite the warnings of icebergs ahead.

Tonight Calamai decided to cut his margin of safety. Technically, he should have slowed his ship way down once he entered fog. But his passengers expected to arrive early the next day in the United States. He had slowed the engines a little, but not enough to put his ship seriously behind schedule. There wouldn't be any trouble. *Andrea Doria* was equipped with the most modern radar, with an officer always stationed at the radar set. The set's range was twenty miles. That was more than enough to give Captain Calamai time to alter course if another ship appeared to be coming too close.

By the time Linda Morgan and her sister went to bed, Linda had forgotten her disappointment about not meeting the captain. All she could think about was seeing her father the next day. After their parents turned out the lights, Linda and Joan talked in excited whispers. It took them a long time to get to sleep, but once they nodded off, they slept deeply.

ANDREA DORIA

Linda Morgan awoke lying in a pile of rubble. Her legs hurt horribly — both kneecaps were broken — and she had no idea where she was. Except for her red book of autographs, which still lay beside her, every trace of her stateroom on board the *Andrea Doria* had vanished. She called out for her mother in Spanish. No one answered. Where was her sister? Where were her parents? Where was she?

By an amazing twist of fate, Linda Morgan had awakened on the bow of the S.S. *Stockholm*, which had crashed into the *Andrea Doria* just as the Italian liner emerged from the fog. The *Stockholm*'s bow pierced the *Andrea Doria*'s hull below the bridge, at precisely the spot where the

Cianfarra family were sleeping in cabins 52 and 54. The bow scooped Linda out of bed and took her with it when the *Stockholm* pulled away, leaving a huge hole in the *Andrea Doria*'s side. Linda's little sister Joan was washed into the sea and never found. Her stepfather was so badly injured that he died a few minutes after the collision. Her mother, though hurt and trapped in

(Left) The crumpled bow of the *Stockholm* following the collision. (Above) As dawn approaches, the abandoned *Andrea Doria* awaits her end. (Right) Linda Morgan is carried ashore in a stretcher. (Far right) Edward Morgan visits his daughter in the hospital after her amazing rescue.

wreckage, was eventually rescued. When a crewman from the *Stockholm* finally heard Linda's cries and found her, he at first assumed she was a passenger from his own ship.

Many hours later, when Jane Cianfarra was finally carried to a lifeboat, she believed that she had lost her husband and both her daughters. It was more than a day before she learned that her daughter Linda was alive. Linda's mother never recovered from the ordeal of the sinking and the traumatic loss of her husband and younger daughter. Not many years later, she died on the anniversary of the *Andrea Doria*'s sinking.

It was only because the *Andrea Doria* took eleven hours to sink that almost everyone on the ship was saved — all but forty-six of the 1,706 people on board. Had the ship gone down as fast as the *Titanic*, in two and a half hours, the death toll would have been much higher. But of all those who escaped alive, the story of Linda Morgan was the most amazing. In the days following the rescue, journalists christened her the Miracle Girl.

By dawn, rescue ships circled the *Andrea Doria* while airplanes carrying reporters and news photographers hovered overhead. This made for possibly the best documented shipwreck in history. Roughly eleven hours after the collision, just past 10:00 A.M. on July 26, 1956, the pride of the Italian Line capsized and sank. Harold Trask, a *Boston Herald* photographer who took the final sinking pictures reproduced here, later won a Pulitzer Prize for his record of the *Andrea Doria*'s final moments.

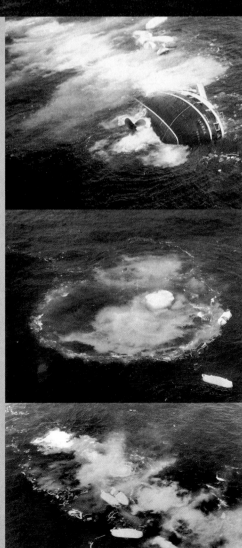

ANDREA DORIA

On the day in the spring of 1995 that I visited the wreck of the *Andrea Doria* the visibility was so poor that she really looked like a ghost. As *NR-1* descended toward the great hull where it lay on its side, I felt as though we were swimming in a snowstorm because of all the sediment in the water. We were about a thousand yards (900 meters) away when the sub's sonar picked up the first faint images of the wreck, but at a hundred feet (30 meters) we still couldn't see a thing. This was getting scary. A slight miscalculation and the sub could snag on a dangling cable or hit a jutting piece of wreckage.

Finally the dim shape of the ship's hull began to appear; this bow was different from the *Titanic*'s, a graceful outward curve rather than a knifelike straight edge. As we came over the bow we could just make out the huge anchor capstans. Then the snowstorm of sediment closed in again and the ship disappeared from view.

Fortunately, we can visit the ship today through the wonderful underwater photographs taken by previous visitors, most of them scuba divers. But I'm not sure I would want to dive on the *Doria* as so many have done. There are too many sharks. And the ship lies at 240 feet (73 meters) — too deep for any but the most experienced diver. Many who have gone down to explore the sunken wreck haven't made it back to the surface alive.

The year the *Andrea Doria* sank was also the year that the jet plane became the most popular way to cross the Atlantic. Within a few years, the great age of the Atlantic liners would be over. The haunting wreck might serve as a fitting memorial to the glory days of those great ships.

Today the *Andrea Doria* lies in 240 feet (73 meters) of water off the island of Nantucket. (Far left) This ship's bell was removed from the stern in the late 1980s. (Left) The wheel from the emergency steering position near the stern. (Below) Like the *Lusitania* wreck, the *Andrea Doria* has also caught the nets of many fishing trawlers.

The Lure of the Ghost Liners

April 14, 1998

If you could have floated high above the North Atlantic half an hour before midnight on April 14, 1912, you would have seen a magical sight. A huge ship, glittering with a thousand lights, glides powerfully across a sea as smooth as glass. Above you the stars twinkle in a completely clear, moonless void. The scene seems perfect until you look ahead. Directly in the liner's path stretches a giant field of ice. And between the ice field and the ship, dotting the dark sea, there are pale masses that look like shadowy mountains — icebergs.

A few minutes later, you see the ship heading straight for one of the bergs. It slowly starts to turn — will it make it? No. The ship's side gently grazes the floating mountain. Great chunks of ice fall onto the deck. At first it seems that no harm has been done — until the ship begins to slow down and then gradually drifts to a stop. But still you see no sign of distress.

EPILOGUE

Then, with a flash that reminds you of the most spectacular holiday fireworks, the first rocket lights up the night.

Over the next two hours, you watch in fascination as the ship's bow sinks steadily into the sea. One lifeboat pulls away, then another. As the stern rises and the deck slopes more steeply, tiny figures leap into the water. The stern rises higher still. Hundreds of people still cling to the ship. Finally the stern points straight up. After remaining motionless for one endless, heart-stopping moment, it slips out of sight. That is how we now see the tragedy of the *Titanic* — as if from a great distance.

More than seventy years would pass before human eyes would gaze on the *Titanic* again. And it's been over ten years since I first dived down to the wreck in a tiny submarine. During those years, I've seen the wrecks and learned the histories of the other great Atlantic liners that disappeared before their time. Of these I remember especially the once-proud *Lusitania*, mangled almost beyond recognition, and the *Titanic*'s sister ship, the *Britannic*, so perfectly preserved she made me think of a bride dressed in her wedding gown who never quite made it to the altar. These and the other ghost liners have become real to me.

Like those tiny figures on the doomed *Titanic*, the people who lived and died on these ships still seem incredibly distant, inhabitants of a lost world. One way of getting closer to them is to put ourselves in their places and to imagine how we would have behaved as our huge and powerful ship that had seemed so safe began to sink. If I had been a young boy traveling third class on the *Titanic*, like Willie Coutts, would I have panicked — or somehow reached safety? If I had been a Sea Scout on the *Britannic*, like James Vickers, would I have

jumped into the first lifeboat or stayed until the ship was about to sink? If I had been asleep on one ship and awakened on another — like Linda Morgan on the *Andrea Doria* — how would it have affected the way I lived the rest of my life?

Despite the many years that have passed

since the sinkings of the *Titanic*, the *Empress of Ireland*, the *Lusitania*, the *Britannic* and the *Andrea Doria*, their stories seem to fascinate us more than ever. Maybe they remind us of a truth that seems more important than ever as we reach the end of the twentieth century: Whenever human beings put too much faith in technology, they regret having done so. Each of the ghost liners chronicled in this book sank, at least in part, because the people who built and sailed them believed they were unsinkable. Both the *Empress of Ireland* and the *Britannic* were sailing with their portholes open, ignoring standard safety precautions. The captain of the *Lusitania* didn't bother to steer

I'm as big a fan of technical achievement as anyone. After all, I have played a role in taking underwater exploration into the space age. But I don't put my final faith in machines. I put my faith in people. The *Titanic* and the other ghost liners teach us that those who trust too much in their own creations will sooner or

the required zigzag pattern even though he knew he was in an area where enemy submarines often lurked. The skipper of the *Andrea Doria* barely slowed down in fog because he put too much faith in his radar. And the *Titanic*, as we know too well, was sailing at full speed despite repeated warnings of icebergs ahead.

later run into an iceberg. In our own time, the iceberg may be a continent-wide power blackout or a nuclear meltdown. Because of the powerful impact of the stories of these lost ships, I have a feeling that people will still be reading about them long after I'm gone, and long after the wrecks we explored have crumbled and disappeared.

Glossary

A-DECK, B-DECK: The *Titanic*, and many other liners, named their decks alphabetically. The top deck was the boat deck, the next one down A-deck, then B-deck and so on downward.

AFT: Toward the back of a ship.

BOAT DECK: The deck of a ship on which lifeboats are carried.

BOILER: A large, coal-burning furnace that boiled water to create the steam which powered a ship like the *Titanic*.

BOW: The front end of a ship.

BRIDGE: The raised platform near the front end of a ship from which it is navigated.

DAVITS: Crane-like arms used for holding and lowering lifeboats.

DEBRIS FIELD: An area around the wreck of a ship where many objects from the ship can be found.

DOCKING BRIDGE: A raised area on the stern of a ship with steering mechanisms, used while the ship is leaving or approaching a pier.

FORWARD: Toward the front of a ship.

LIST: When a ship is leaning to one side or the other.

MINE: A floating explosive device designed to blow up on contact with ships.

PORT: The left-hand side of a ship when facing forward.

PROMENADE: An upper deck on a ship where passengers may walk.

PROW: The tip of a ship's bow.

STARBOARD: The right-hand side of ship when facing the bow.

STERN: The rear end of a ship.

TELEGRAPH: An instrument on a ship's bridge used to send messages to the engine room.

Recommended Further Reading

Exploring the Titanic
by Robert D. Ballard
1988 (Scholastic [U.S. and Canada]).
•Robert Ballard's gripping account of the search for and discovery of the *Titanic*.

Inside the Titanic
by Ken Marschall and Hugh Brewster 1997 (Little, Brown and Company [U.S. and Canada]; Allen & Unwin [Australia])
•A large-format illustrated book featuring cut-away illustrations revealing the ship's interiors.

On Board the Titanic
by Shelley Tanaka 1995 (Hyperion [U.S.]; Scholastic [Canada])

•What it was really like to be on the *Titanic* the night it went down, as seen through the eyes of two young survivors, Jack Thayer and Harold Bride.

Polar the Titanic Bear
by Daisy Corning Spedden 1994 (Little, Brown and Company)
•A first-hand account of the sinking, written by survivor Daisy Corning Spedden for her son, telling the story of their adventures through the eyes of his toy bear, Polar.

A Night to Remember
by Walter Lord 1955 (Bantam Books)

•One of the best accounts of the sinking of the *Titanic*, by an author who interviewed many of the survivors. (Adult reading level.)

Good Reference Books with an Adult Reading Level

The Discovery of the Titanic
by Robert D. Ballard 1987 (Warner Books [U.S.]; Penguin [Canada]; Allen and Unwin [Australia]).
•The original account of Ballard's search for the *Titanic*, its discovery and his subsequent exploration of the ship, featuring hundreds of exciting underwater photographs.

Exploring the Lusitania
by Robert D. Ballard with Spencer Dunmore 1993 (Warner Books [U.S. and Canada]; Weidenfeld and Nicolson [Australia]).
•Robert Ballard's account of the tragic final voyage of the *Lusitania*, and his investigations to discover what really sank the ship.

Lost Liners
by Robert D. Ballard and Rick Archbold 1997 (Hyperion [U.S.]; Little, Brown [Canada]; Allen and Unwin [Australia].
•A detailed illustrated history of the Atlantic passenger liners told through the famous wrecked ships that Robert Ballard has explored.

Titanic: An Illustrated History
by Don Lynch 1992 (Hyperion [U.S.]; Penguin [Canada]; Hodder Headline PLC [Australia]).
•An excellent illustrated account of the *Titanic*'s brief life, and her tragic end, featuring hundreds of rare photographs and numerous paintings by maritime artist Ken Marschall.

Prints and posters of Ken Marschall's work are available from:
Trans-Atlantic Designs, Inc.
P.O. Box 539
Redondo Beach, CA. 90277   U.S.A.
e-mail: tadesigns@aol.com

Picture Credits

Cover images: Ken Marschall.
Endpapers: Ulster Folk and Transport Museum.
1   Painting by Ken Marschall.
2-3   Painting by Ken Marschall.
4-5   Painting by Ken Marschall.

PROLOGUE:
FROM *TITANIC* TO *BRITANNIC*

6   (Left) C.K. Peters, courtesy of Odyssey Corporation. (Right) C.K. Peters, courtesy of Odyssey Corporation.
6-7   C.K. Peters, courtesy of Odyssey Corporation.
8-9   Painting by Ken Marschall.

CHAPTER ONE:
GHOST LINER

10   Painting by Ken Marschall.
11   (Top) Woods Hole Oceanographic Institute (WHOI). (Bottom) WHOI.
12   (Top) Painting by Ken Marschall. (Second from top) Painting by Ken Marschall. (Middle) Painting by Ken Marschall. (Second from bottom) Painting by Ken Marschall. (Bottom) Painting by Ken Marschall.
12   (Bottom right) WHOI.
12-13   Painting by Ken Marschall.
13   (Bottom left) WHOI. (Bottom right) WHOI.
14   Painting by Ken Marschall.
15   (Left) WHOI. (Center) WHOI. (Right) Photograph courtesy of Barbara Kharouf.
16-17   Painting by Ken Marschall.
17   (Top left) Don Lynch Collection. (Top right) WHOI. (Inset) The Margaret Strong Museum. (Bottom left) WHOI. (Bottom right) WHOI.
18   (Top left) WHOI. (Top middle) WHOI. (Top right) WHOI. (Middle) Diagram by Ken Marschall. (Bottom left) WHOI. (Bottom right) WHOI.
19   WHOI.

CHAPTER TWO:
FOURTEEN MINUTES OF TERROR

20-21   Mark Reynolds Collection.
22   Photograph by Gary Gentile.
23   (Left bottom) Photograph by Gary Gentile. (Right top) Mark Reynolds Collection. (Right upper) Corbis-Bettmann, U13684 INP. (Right lower) Philippe Beaudry Collection. (Bottom) Mark Reynolds Collection.

24   (Top) Hulton Getty Collection. (Bottom left) *Collier's* magazine, Mark Reynolds Collection. (Bottom right) Corbis-Bettmann Collection, U13688 INP.
25   (Left) Mary Evans Picture Library. (Right) Diagrams by Jack McMaster.
26   Photograph courtesy of Gordon E. Martyn.
26-27   Painting by Ken Marschall.
27   (Top left) Photograph by Gary Gentile. (Top right) Photograph by Gary Gentile.

CHAPTER THREE:
CASUALTY OF WAR

28-29   Painting by Ken Marschall.
30   Painting by Ken Marschall.
30   Eric Sauder Collection.
30-31   Painting by Ken Marschall.
32   (Left) Brown Brothers. (Right) Stanford University. (Bottom left) Eric Sauder Collection.
33   Jonathan Blair © National Geographic Society.
34   Diagrams by Jack McMaster.
34-35   Painting by Ken Marschall.
35   (Left) Photograph by Gary Gentile. (Right) Photograph by Gary Gentile.
36   (Left) Jonathan Blair © National Geographic Society. (Right) Jonathan Blair © National Geographic Society.
36-37   Painting by Ken Marschall.
37   (Left) Jonathan Blair © National Geographic Society. (Right) Jonathan Blair © National Geographic Society.

CHAPTER FOUR:
INNOCENT VICTIM

38   Painting by Ken Marschall.
39   (Top) Karen Kamuda Collection. (Bottom) Titanic Historical Society.
40   (Top) Ken Marschall Collection. (Lower left) Ulster Folk and Transport Museum, H2150A, Simon Mills Collection. (Lower right) Simon Mills Collection.
41   (Top) Simon Mills Collection. (Middle) National Maritime Museum, Simon Mills Collection. (Bottom) George E. Pearce Collection.
42-43   Painting by Ken Marschall.

Acknowledgments

Robert Ballard wishes to thank everyone who has gone exploring with me over what is now more than ten years of searching the ocean depths. A special thanks as well to the National Geographic Society, for its key support on so many of my expeditions.

Ken Marschall wishes to thank Madison Press for their continued confidence in, and enthusiasm for, his artwork, Bob Ballard and the Woods Hole Oceanographic Institution for access to their vast archive of *Titanic* wreck photographs, and Vern Shrock for his support and encouragement

Rick Archbold wishes to thank, first, Don Lynch, Simon Mills, Mark Reynolds and Eric Sauder, four liner experts who guided my research and read the text for accuracy.

Thanks also to the following: Sarah Whitehouse of CineNova Productions, who acted as emissary for Linda Morgan; Linda Morgan for consenting to read my version of her harrowing experience on the *Andrea Doria*; Barbara Kharouf, for information about and the photograph of her father Willie Coutts; Dr. Gordon E. Martyn, who lent us a picture of his mother Grace Hanagan; Frank Grisbook of Scouts Canada, who put us in touch with George E. Pearce, fountain of information on the role of British Sea Scouts during World War I.

Finally, kudos to the team at Madison Press: Ian R. Coutts, whose astute editing is always leavened with a love for all things nautical; Sandra Hall, who never misses a production detail; Hugh Brewster, for having the idea in the first place.

DESIGN AND ART DIRECTION:
Gordon Sibley Design Inc.

EDITORIAL DIRECTOR:
Hugh M. Brewster

PROJECT EDITOR:
Ian R. Coutts

EDITORIAL ASSISTANCE:
Susan Aihoshi

PRODUCTION DIRECTOR:
Susan Barrable

PRODUCTION CO-ORDINATOR:
Sandra L. Hall

COLOR SEPARATION:
Colour Technologies

PRINTING AND BINDING:
T.W.P. America, Inc.

Ghost Liners was produced by
Madison Press Books,
which is under the direction of Albert E. Cummings.